W9-CIR-697

ANDREW JACKSON

The Presidents of the United States

George Washington
1789–1797

John Adams
1797–1801

Thomas Jefferson
1801–1809

James Madison
1809–1817

James Monroe
1817–1825

John Quincy Adams
1825–1829

Andrew Jackson
1829–1837

Martin Van Buren
1837–1841

William Henry Harrison
1841

John Tyler
1841–1845

James Polk
1845–1849

Zachary Taylor
1849–1850

Millard Fillmore
1850–1853

Franklin Pierce
1853–1857

James Buchanan
1857–1861

Abraham Lincoln
1861–1865

Andrew Johnson
1865–1869

Ulysses S. Grant
1869–1877

Rutherford B. Hayes
1877–1881

James Garfield
1881

Chester Arthur
1881–1885

Grover Cleveland
1885–1889

Benjamin Harrison
1889–1893

Grover Cleveland
1893–1897

William McKinley
1897–1901

Theodore Roosevelt
1901–1909

William H. Taft
1909–1913

Woodrow Wilson
1913–1921

Warren Harding
1921–1923

Calvin Coolidge
1923–1929

Herbert Hoover
1929–1933

Franklin D. Roosevelt
1933–1945

Harry Truman
1945–1953

Dwight Eisenhower
1953–1961

John F. Kennedy
1961–1963

Lyndon B. Johnson
1963–1969

Richard Nixon
1969–1974

Gerald Ford
1974–1977

Jimmy Carter
1977–1981

Ronald Reagan
1981–1989

George H. W. Bush
1989–1993

William J. Clinton
1993–2001

George W. Bush
2001–2009

Barack Obama
2009–

Presidents and Their Times

ANDREW JACKSON

KATIE MARSICO

Marshall Cavendish
Benchmark
New York

Published by Marshall Cavendish Benchmark
An imprint of Marshall Cavendish Corporation

Website: www.marshallcavendish.us

This publication represents the opinions and views of the author based on Katie Marsico's personal
experience, knowledge, and research. The information in this book serves as a general guide only.
The author and publisher have used their best efforts in preparing this book and disclaim liability
rising directly and indirectly from the use and application of this book.

Other Marshall Cavendish Offices:
Marshall Cavendish International (Asia) Private Limited, 1 New Industrial Road, Singapore 536196 •
Marshall Cavendish International (Thailand) Co Ltd. 253 Asoke, 12th Flr, Sukhumvit 21 Road, Klongtoey
Nua, Wattana, Bangkok 10110, Thailand • Marshall Cavendish (Malaysia) Sdn Bhd, Times Subang, Lot
46, Subang Hi-Tech Industrial Park, Batu Tiga, 40000 Shah Alam, Selangor Darul Ehsan, Malaysia

Marshall Cavendish is a trademark of Times Publishing Limited

All websites were available and accurate when this book was sent to press.

Library of Congress Cataloging-in-Publication Data

Marsico, Katie, 1980–
Andrew Jackson / by Katie Marsico.
p. cm. — (Presidents and their times)
Includes bibliographical references and index.
Summary: "Provides comprehensive information on President Andrew Jackson and places him within his
historical and cultural context. Also explored are the formative events of his times and how he
responded" — Provided by publisher.
ISBN 978-0-7614-4813-6
1. Jackson, Andrew, 1767–1845—Juvenile literature. 2. Presidents—United States—
Biography—Juvenile literature. I. Title.
E3821.M373 2011
973.5'6092—dc22
[B]
2009011878

Editor: Christine Florie
Publisher: Michelle Bisson
Art Director: Anahid Hamparian
Series Designer: Alex Ferrari

Photo research by Thomas Khoo

The photographs in this book are used by permission and through the courtesy of: *Corbis:* 24, 49, 56,
70, 81, 87; *Getty Images:* 37, 92 (r); *North Wind Picture Archives:* 10, 12, 13, 18, 26, 30, 80, 92 (l);
Photolibrary: 8, 11, 33, 34, 45, 46, 50, 58, 67, 69, 73, 85, 93 (l); *Topfoto:* cover, 3, 6, 14, 16, 17, 28, 31,
35, 40, 41, 42, 55, 57, 63, 64, 68, 72, 78, 83, 83, 91, 93 (r).

Printed in Malaysia
1 3 5 6 4 2

CONTENTS

Andrew Jackson served as America's seventh president.

A Spirited Start in a Changing Nation

Andrew Jackson is a pivotal figure in American history, a man whose life and work meant many things to his countrymen, past and present. He was a patriot, a successful general, and a determined president. He was admired for his devotion to the welfare of ordinary citizens, but he was not without his share of faults. His quick temper and his lack of patience antagonized many people. While president, he had a troubled relationship with Congress, and his controversial decisions, especially his treatment of American Indians, continue to be criticized.

Yet the passionate red-headed boy who grew up along America's frontier in the late eighteenth century also became the voice for other frontier people, people who were largely overlooked by those individuals who held political and social authority. Jackson saw to the interests of average farmers and laborers, helped shape the beliefs and interests of the **Democratic Party**, and did not hesitate to act courageously and aggressively to protect his country both on the battlefield and in the White House. From a young age he overcame many hardships and resolutely worked his way to the highest office in the nation. Along the way he displayed many of the qualities of leadership that Americans continue to admire.

From a Family of Frontiersmen

Jackson's early years were not always easy. About two years before he was born, his parents, Andrew Jackson and Elizabeth

Andrew Jackson was born in this log cabin in the Waxhaws of the Carolinas.

Hutchinson Jackson, left northern Ireland to settle in colonial America. When they reached their new home in 1765, the couple already had two sons: a two-year-old, Hugh, and a five-month-old, Robert. Like many other Europeans who crossed the Atlantic during the eighteenth century, they were eager to make a fresh start and to seek opportunities for wealth and freedom in a new land.

Andrew and Elizabeth Jackson were practical people. They realized that their goals would not be accomplished overnight or without determination, bravery, and hard work. The Jacksons began their pioneer adventure traveling the Catawba Trail, which stretched from Pennsylvania to the Carolinas. They purchased about 200 acres of land along an area known as Twelve Mile Creek in the Waxhaws, a frontier region that overlapped the western part of the border of the North and South Carolina colonies. There the Jacksons built a log home and planned to farm the land.

Yet, Andrew's father worked with soil that was not ideal for growing crops; he also had to clear his property of trees that stood in the way of planting the fields. The young Irishman was not easily frustrated by hard labor, however. In the summer of 1766 Elizabeth became pregnant again. Near the end of the following winter, Andrew fatally injured himself while trying to move a log. The twenty-nine-year-old frontiersman died shortly before his third son was born on March 15, 1767. The infant was given his father's name.

Widowed and forced to care for three young sons on her own, Elizabeth took shelter in the home of her sister, Jane Crawford, who lived on a nearby farm with her husband, Robert, and their eight children. Not long afterward, Jane died, and Jackson's mother assumed responsibility for tending to the entire brood of youngsters. The Jackson boys were each expected to earn their keep by performing a variety of daily chores, which included chopping wood, fetching water, and feeding livestock.

Elizabeth was eager that her family receive a proper education. She was hopeful that Andrew would one day become a minister and did her part to further this dream by dutifully reading to him and the other children in her care from the Bible. She also made sure they attended schools that taught lessons in Latin and Greek. Yet Elizabeth's best attempts to shape Andrew into a serious and refined young man were often challenged by the boy's untamed personality.

As a boy, Andrew preferred playing outside to studying in the classroom.

Andrew was naturally impatient and clearly preferred sports and physical activities to school lessons. While he excelled in areas such as horseback riding, wrestling, and racing, he showed little talent for spelling, science, and history. Tall, handsome, and strong, he never failed to impress his friends with his athletic abilities. His teachers, meanwhile, were not pleased by his performance in the classroom.

"I could throw him three times out of four, but he never stayed throwed," one boyhood acquaintance later recalled of the future president's knack for wrestling. "He was dead game even then and never would give up." Despite his obvious preference for the playing field over the schoolhouse, however, Andrew gained a reputation for being an exceptional reader as a child. This proved an important skill inside the classroom and also in his community. Many frontiersmen in the Waxhaws were not literate and so looked to Andrew when a newspaper or official notice needed to be read. Before he even reached his teens, the youth gained valuable experience that would one day help him in a career involving public speaking and seeing to the interests of men and women who did not have much wealth or education.

Beginning in about 1776, Andrew got a taste of the political excitement that shaped the nation he would ultimately lead. That summer the colonies formally declared independence from Great Britain. Though his early involvement in the Revolutionary War (1775–1783) was limited to sharing newspaper reports about the conflict with his fellow frontiersmen, Andrew soon proved his dedication to America in a more daring fashion.

Patriotism in Spite of Pain

While skirmishes during the first few years of the war rarely reached the Waxhaws, the majority of Carolinians who dwelled in Andrew's region nonetheless supported the cause of the Continental Army, which was led by General George Washington. Most colonists wanted relief from what they saw as steep taxes,

George Washington led the Continental Army during the Revolutionary War.

Patriots lead a loyalist out of their village.

unfair laws, and interference from a mother country far across the Atlantic. The smaller number of individuals who remained loyal to Great Britain were called **Loyalists** or **Tories**.

For frontiersmen like Andrew and his kin, the decision of what side to choose was clear. Most of these strong-willed men and women had journeyed from faraway countries and had made a living out of battling the American wilderness to create a better existence. They sought opportunities that they had been lacking in other nations, and the threat of Great Britain limiting their success and happiness in their new homes was disturbing. It was therefore no surprise that the Jacksons were among many Waxhaws clans who pledged their alliance to **patriot** ideals.

When the fighting reached South Carolina in 1779, several members of Andrew's family became involved in the conflict. His uncle Robert headed a **militia** that was chosen to defend Charleston, South Carolina. Andrew's brother, Hugh, though only sixteen at the time, proudly joined its ranks. Tragedy struck in May 1780, however, when the British captured Charleston, and Hugh was killed in combat.

Patriots battling British forces in the Waxhaws.

The frontier community was plagued with further tragedies in the weeks that followed. As British forces triumphed over the Continental Army, Waxhaw residents witnessed their share of suffering, dying, and brutality. Elizabeth and her remaining sons helped care for wounded patriots in their area, but tending to injured colonists was not enough to satisfy Andrew. He passionately believed in the patriot cause, and he was enraged at the enemy who had taken his brother's life. For these reasons—and despite the fact that Andrew was only thirteen—in the summer of 1780, he also joined the South Carolina militia, along with his brother Robert.

Since Andrew was just a teenager, he was designated a messenger. Andrew took his responsibilities seriously though and was proud to serve the patriots. He witnessed a few skirmishes and battles and, even if he did not actively participate, he never abandoned his duties for fear of being too close to bloodshed or watching men die. In fact, a young girl who saw Andrew riding down a country road later reported how, when she asked him of the colonists' progress against the British, he enthusiastically informed her, "Oh, we are popping them still!"

Andrew did not change his attitude when he and Robert were captured during a British raid on the Waxhaws in 1781. When Andrew refused to clean the boots of a British officer, the soldier slashed the boy's face and hand with a curved sword called a saber. He and Robert were later forced to march 40 miles to a prison in Camden, South Carolina, where they were fed little and fell ill with smallpox.

Luckily for the Jackson brothers and several of their fellow prisoners, Elizabeth proved as courageous as they were. After

A British officer attacks young Andrew with a saber.

A Mother's Last Words

Decades after his mother's death, Jackson recalled her final message to him as she left the Waxhaws for the last time in the fall of 1781. "Almost her last words to me when about to start for Charleston . . . were 'Andrew . . . in this world, you have to make your own way.' . . . As things turned out, I might as well have been penniless, as I already was homeless and friendless. The memory of my mother and her teachings were, after all, the only capital I had to start in life with, and on that capital I have made my way." Andrew's later actions demonstrated how dearly he took her wisdom to heart.

pleading with the British officers in charge of Camden, she managed to arrange for the release of her sons and some of the other patriots being held there. The trek back to the Waxhaws was difficult. Andrew and Robert were desperately ill and lacked decent clothes to shelter them from the heavy rain. Succumbing to his sickness, Robert died a few days after the family's return. Elizabeth was able to revive Andrew, but his recovery took several months. He had become, in his own words, "a skeleton—not quite 6 feet long and a little over 6 inches thick!"

By the fall of 1781 Elizabeth was convinced that Andrew was well on the road to improved health, and so she departed from the Waxhaws to nurse American soldiers suffering from cholera aboard enemy ships in Charleston Harbor. Sadly she herself caught the infection and died shortly after her arrival. Andrew suddenly found himself an orphan in difficult and uncertain circumstances.

FROM ROWDY LAD TO RESPECTED LAWYER

Although Andrew Jackson had grown up on the frontier, Elizabeth had always been there to provide guidance, stability, and love. Without her, the teenager found life in the Waxhaws difficult and lonely. He moved in with relatives, but his living arrangements never lasted very long.

Though clearly intelligent and brave, Jackson's temper often got the better of him. His tendency to become quickly angered was often at the root of violent arguments with members of his family. As a result of this constant tension with his relatives, Jackson shuffled from home to home. In 1782 he packed up his belongings and headed to Charleston, South Carolina.

Jackson moved to Charleston, South Carolina, in 1782.

The fifteen-year-old's time in Charleston was filled with self-indulgent, rowdy behavior. As the Revolutionary War drew to a close, Jackson had no apparent career plans. He and his friends spent the majority of their time gambling and drinking—activities that the young men became even more deeply involved in when

Jackson indulged in drinking and other rowdy behavior while in Charleston.

Jackson suddenly received a small inheritance from a grandfather in Ireland. Jackson spent part of this unexpected fortune on a gold watch, new pistols, elegant clothes, a fine horse, and lodging in an expensive Charleston hotel.

Jackson's love of betting, drinking, dancing, and carelessly spending money with his companions ate away at the inheritance. It was not long before Jackson was in serious debt—an offense that was punishable by a prison sentence during that era in U.S. history. Luck was on his side, however, as he cast the dice one final time to try to recover some of his losses. Jackson won enough to repay his debts, but the experience made him realize that his wild ways in Charleston could not continue.

In 1783 he returned home to the Waxhaws and boarded with former neighbors while he attempted to settle down and become a schoolteacher. Jackson, however, found life in his old community far from fulfilling. As one local later described him, he was "the most roaring, rollicking . . . horse-racing, card-playing,

Life as a teacher did not suit Jackson.

mischievous fellow that ever lived." Though Jackson understood that it was impractical to do nothing but gamble and attend parties, instructing students was not enough to satisfy his desire for adventure and his growing ambition to make a name for himself in the world. In 1784 he therefore departed the Waxhaws and traveled to Salisbury, North Carolina.

PRACTICING LAW AS A PIONEER

Jackson saw his move to Salisbury as a fresh start and the opportunity to establish himself. The town was the county seat of

Rowan County and an ideal place to launch a legal career, as many lawyers and politicians lived and worked there. Jackson knew that he had the quick-wittedness and reading skills needed to practice law, and the profession was a promising pathway for a man who one day hoped to succeed in politics. To become an attorney, however, he first had to find a more experienced lawyer under whom he could study the field.

A local professional named Spruce McKay took Jackson under his wing not long after he arrived in Salisbury and proved to be an excellent teacher. In the late 1700s this system of training essentially served as a substitute for modern-day law school. Although some of the work Jackson did for McKay, such as running errands and sweeping the floor, was unrelated to his education, he still learned a great deal about the law. He copied legal documents for McKay, and he observed his mentor dealing with clients. The preparation Jackson received enabled him to start his own practice in September 1787.

A new career did not completely put an end to Jackson's wild antics, however. Local ladies regarded him as "quite a beau in the town," and his male friends were constantly entertained by his hard-drinking ways and mischievous sense of humor. The tall, dashing Jackson was charmingly energetic and quickly proved himself both a favorite at balls and the genius behind countless practical jokes. Though the twenty-one-year-old attorney was an ideal companion in taverns and at dancing parties, however, he struggled to attract clients. The area was already filled with several older and more established lawyers who made it difficult for Jackson to impress locals seeking legal representation.

The Jackson That Used to Live in Salisbury

Despite Jackson's popularity, few Salisbury residents could have foreseen his political success. His personality did not remind many people of the dignified, proper politicians of whom they had read. One townswoman exclaimed years later when she heard he was running for president, "Jackson up for president? Jackson? Andrew Jackson? The Jackson that used to live in Salisbury. . . . Well, if Andrew Jackson can be president, anybody can!"

As a result, Jackson jumped at the chance to serve as an attorney for the western district of North Carolina when it arose. He was offered the position by an old acquaintance, John McNairy, who was also the superior court judge for that portion of the frontier. Not all young lawyers would have been so eager to accept a post in the western district, which stretched west toward the Mississippi River and included parts of present-day Tennessee. It was largely unsettled land that faced all the challenges of an untamed wilderness, including raids by American Indian and lawlessness.

Unafraid of life on the frontier, Jackson saw the opportunity to act as a public prosecutor, or **solicitor general**, in the western district as a means to distinguish himself. He reasoned that, as America's boundaries continued to move westward, settlers would make their homes closer to the Mississippi River, and these men and women would inevitably require the legal help that he could offer. He also realised that he was clearly not advancing his career in eastern North Carolina.

In the spring of 1788 Jackson, McNairy, and a group of fellow lawyers who were likewise looking for success on the far side of the Cumberland Mountains headed west. They planned on beginning their practice in Nashville, Tennessee, which was then regarded as little more than a disorganized frontier village. Along the way the party made stops in Jonesboro, Tennessee, and other such towns, where the travelers temporarily settled and worked in local district courts.

Although Jackson was able to gain more trial experience there than he ever had in the eastern Carolinas, he still encountered more seasoned attorneys who were scornful of his newness to the field. Colonel Waightstill Avery, who had opposed him during one case in Jonesboro, was such an individual. The older man poked fun at the youthful prosecutor's frequent need to refer to legal books while in the courtroom, but the humor in the situation was completely lost on Jackson.

"Sir: When a man's feelings and [character] and feelings are injured, he ought to seek a speedy redress," Jackson wrote in a note filled with fiery tones in August 1788. "My [character] you have injured, and further, you have insulted me in the presence of a court and a large [audience]. I therefore call upon you as a gentleman to give me satisfaction for the same." What the twenty-one-year-old lawyer was demanding of Avery was the chance to defend his honor in a duel. During that period in American history—and especially in less-settled sections of the country—pistol duels were a common method of resolving disagreements. For Jackson it was more important than ever that he be taken seriously as a gentleman and an attorney on the western frontier. He was eager to put his past as a wild and reckless youth behind him and did not feel he could afford to be the subject of anyone's mockery.

Though both lawyers proceeded with the duel, no one was actually injured. The purpose of such displays was often far less about murdering someone than regaining public honor, which Jackson saw as essential to moving ahead in the world. Nor would it be long before he began to do just that. In a matter of months he reached Nashville, where he was able to further his career as an attorney as well as demonstrate his political potential.

A New Life and Love in Nashville

From the moment Jackson and McNair headed for Nashville in September 1788, chaos and lawlessness seemed to shape their adventures. The men narrowly escaped a raid by Cherokee Indians before arriving in the somewhat disorganized frontier village the following October. It would be another eight years before Tennessee officially entered the Union as a state in 1796, and, in the meantime, Nashville was anything but orderly and sophisticated.

Apart from the stark layout of the town—which mainly consisted of a few stores, taverns, houses, tents, wooden shacks and a rundown log courthouse—few residents seemed to have much regard for the law. Debt was widespread, and men and women who were owed money were often too fearful of the debtors to try to collect it. As Jackson knew from experience, a frontier existence was undeniably difficult, but it was made even harder when individuals used intimidation and violence to create their own laws.

Yet the newly arrived prosecutor was not easily scared. Jackson immediately ordered that all debts be paid and did not back down when some of the debtors in question protested his efforts. On the contrary, Jackson responded to one offender who stomped on his foot by hitting the man with a chunk of wood.

The people of Nashville quickly realized that Jackson was not only a man with deep professional determination but also a pioneer who was unafraid of using whatever means were necessary to hold his ground. The number of Jackson's clients soon grew, though not all of them had the money to pay him with actual currency. Some offered him land in exchange for his legal services. Jackson usually welcomed such trades, as they greatly increased his property holdings in the area.

Despite his growing wealth, however, Jackson did not immediately build an estate on his own land. When he first arrived in Nashville, he boarded with a famous local family, the Donelsons, who had played an important role in founding the town. He soon became interested in young Rachel Donelson Robards. The same age as Jackson, Rachel had also grown up on the frontier. She was delicate, charming, and lovely, despite having endured all the difficult experiences of a pioneer.

One relative, described her by saying, "She was irresistible to men"; another concluded that she was "the best storyteller, the best dancer, the sprightliest companion, [and] the most dashing horsewoman in the Western country." Rachel's appeal caused her first husband, Lewis Robards, to be jealous. The couple had lived together in Kentucky, but Rachel returned to Nashville when the marriage soured.

Rachel met Jackson when she returned home, and the two fell in love. Yet she was still a married woman at the time. However, Robards began divorce proceedings in 1790. Having been told that the marriage was officially over in the winter of that year, Rachel and Jackson wed in August 1791. Although a scandal would later arise surrounding their marriage, the union was a happy one. As the future president would say in the years to come, "Heaven will not be heaven to me if I do not meet my wife there."

YOUNG POLITICIAN AND POPULAR SOLDIER

Three

Andrew and Rachel Jackson returned from a Mississippi honeymoon to begin their life together. In late 1793 however they were informed that Rachel's marriage to Robards had only officially ended in September of that year. While the pair had believed that a finalized divorce was granted in 1791, Rachel's first husband had, in fact, simply gained permission to file for one at that time. Jackson and Rachel were remarried in January 1794, though scandal surrounding the misunderstanding continued to haunt him as his career won him increasing public attention.

Jackson was already famous for his abilities as a prosecutor throughout Nashville, where he and Rachel took up residence on

The Jacksons owned a 330-acre estate in Nashville.

a 330-acre estate. Ordinary citizens as well as experienced law-makers regarded him as brave, determined, and dedicated to his profession and family. As her husband's prospects on the frontier flourished, Rachel also gained a reputation for her skills as a homemaker and land manager. With Jackson frequently away on business, she oversaw the majority of their household affairs, in addition to the day-to-day responsibilities connected with their cotton plantation. Rachel's efficiency at such tasks allowed the then-twenty-nine-year-old lawyer to further his ambitions in Nashville. New opportunities to advance presented themselves by June 1, 1796, when Tennessee entered the Union as the sixteenth state. When the former frontier territory was required to send **delegates** to Congress, Jackson ran for a seat in the **House of Representatives** and won. Despite his fearlessness and practicality, the young politician still had much to learn about how business was conducted in Philadelphia, Pennsylvania, which was then the nation's capital.

Already a landmark, this eastern city was far more developed than any pioneer town in which Jackson had lived. People dressed in the latest fashions, and men and women who held places in society generally carried themselves in a reserved and dignified manner. Any qualities Jackson had that may have impressed the townsfolk in Nashville did not so quickly win over the Philadelphians with whom he became better acquainted in December 1796.

One fellow congressman, Albert Gallatin, described Jackson as "a tall, lank, uncouth-looking personage, with long locks of hair hanging over his face . . . his dress singular [and] his manners and deportment those of a rough backwoodsman." The contrast between the youthful westerner and the polished gentlemen

Historic Philadephia was remarkably different from the Tennessee frontier Jackson knew so well.

who regularly spoke in Congress on weighty issues of the day was obvious to everyone, including Jackson. He often wisely kept silent and observed how other members of the House of Representatives addressed various political challenges. Although he was a naturally passionate person who did not hesitate to speak his mind in the courtrooms of Nashville, he was smart enough to realize that—as of the mid–1790s—he lacked the experience to play a leading role in the meeting halls of Philadelphia.

Nevertheless, Jackson refused to back down from a career in American politics. By the time he won a seat in the U.S. Senate in the fall of 1797, he had learned the customs of Congress and knew what was needed to earn respect as a politician and as a member of Philadelphia society. He even had a local tailor design him a fashionable new suit to wear before the Senate met that year. In some ways, however, Jackson was clearly unwilling to adapt.

More comfortable with expressing his political viewpoints after several months in Congress, he was also often unable to abandon the fiery temper and spirited personality that had a lready defined his reputation in other parts of the country. He could certainly be courteous and practical-minded, and few doubted his devotion to the United States. For some Philadelphia politicians, though, it was nearly impossible to perceive Jackson as anything more than a common man from a frontier state who was rough around the edges and in possession of a raw courage that was admirable—but not necessarily well suited for the floor of the U.S. Senate.

As one visitor to the capital remarked of him and his service to Tennessee as a congressman, "That wretched state is very fitly represented." Nor did Jackson particularly enjoy his term as a senator, especially as the job kept him away from Rachel for long stretches of time. Forced to attend to a few financial matters in Nashville, he stepped down from the post in 1798 and returned to Tennessee and his wife. Once at home, he continued to seek new ways to advance his career—a goal that ultimately inter-mingled with his intense determination, fierce sense of honor, and famous set of dueling pistols.

A Dangerous Man

As one of the nation's earliest political leaders and the third president of the United States, Thomas Jefferson (*below*) had the opportunity to observe Jackson as a young statesman. He was not completely impressed by what he saw. In fact, he predicted that Jackson's personality would lead to trouble if the Tennessean was ever placed in a position of real power. "His passions are terrible," Jefferson later recalled. "He could never speak on account of the rashness of his feelings. I have seen him attempt it repeatedly and as often choke with rage. . . . He is a dangerous man."

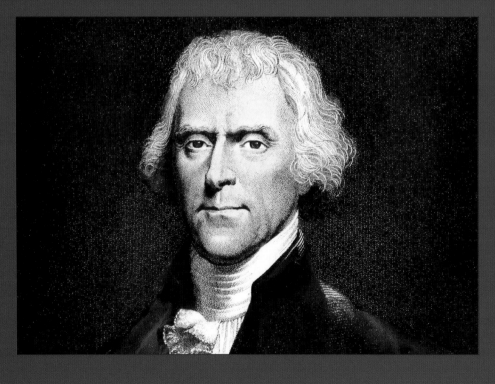

Revered Judge and Renowned Dueler

Jackson did not abandon his reputation building after he stepped down from Philadelphia politics. Shortly after reestablishing himself as a Nashville attorney, he was elected a judge of the Superior Court of Tennessee. In this role Jackson became known for his fair decisions and dedication to upholding the law, even when it meant using his pistols to do so. He did not hesitate to pursue unruly defendants at gunpoint when they showed disrespect in his courtroom.

In many ways this job was quite different from the one in Philadelphia. Jackson was constantly in contact with average

Jackson apprehending an accused criminal while serving as a judge in Tennessee.

men and women with everyday problems. In Tennessee, however, he had the authority to deal with these individuals—and simultaneously further his own career—in a manner that was common to life on the American frontier.

For example, when Jackson was elected a major general of the Tennessee militia in 1802, he became caught up in a bitter political feud with his rival, John Sevier, who was also the state's former governor. Matters intensified when Sevier publicly insulted his opponent in 1803 by proclaiming, "I know of no great service you have rendered the country, except taking a trip to [Mississippi] with another man's wife."

The remark clearly referred to Rachel and Jackson's questionable union in connection to the timing of her divorce from Robards. In response to the insult to his wife, Jackson challenged Sevier to a duel. The pair decided to meet on the other side of the Kentucky border, since dueling was illegal in Tennessee. The match resulted in no more than a few harsh words and a draw of weapons, as friends of both men intervened before a shot could be fired. Just as had been the case with Avery in Jonesboro, though, a lack of bloodshed did not mean a loss of victory. Jackson's display of courage by simply showing up for the duel was enough to defend both his and his wife's reputation against Sevier's taunts.

By 1804, however, Jackson was once more in debt and was forced to sell the large estate on which he and Rachel lived. Serving as a state judge was helpful to Jackson's career but was not necessarily a profitable profession; so the couple had no choice but to make sacrifices. The new home the Jacksons purchased, the Hermitage, would become forever associated with them.

Jackson eventually developed the Hermitage into an established property.

While the Hermitage was no more than a few basic wooden structures on 425 acres of land in 1804, it was soon transformed into a developed property surrounding an elegant brick house. In the years that followed, the Jacksons grew cotton, corn, and wheat on their land. Their working plantation also contained stables and horses, as well as teams of slaves to perform hard labor. As Jackson prospered, he bought a racetrack, too.

This investment led to a conflict in 1806. After Jackson won a horserace against a family called the Dickinsons, a war of words occurred that ended with Jackson challenging Charles Dickinson to a duel. On May 30 both Tennesseans met in Kentucky to defend their honor; unfortunately the episode turned out to be more deadly than any of Jackson's previous experiences with pistols. He fatally shot Dickinson and in turn received a serious chest injury that left him crippled for weeks. Eager to appear confident and courageous, however, Jackson quietly remarked to

Jackson and Dickinson during their duel in 1806.

a friend who stood nearby, "Oh! I believe that he has [wounded] me a little." He then calmly asked that no one make his pain obvious to Dickinson's supporters.

Jackson's convalescence allowed him some additional time with Rachel and their plantation. For a few brief years they enjoyed a calmer, less conflicted existence and even began planning for a family. After the Jacksons learned that Rachel was unable to have children of her own, they adopted a little boy, one of Rachel's brother and sister-in-law's twins, in 1809 and named him Andrew Jackson Jr. In a few years, however, family life at the Hermitage was interrupted by world affairs, and Jackson was granted another chance to serve the nation.

Jackson and his wife adopted Andrew Jackson Jr. in 1809. This portrait was completed when he was an adult.

OLD HICKORY AND NEW HOSTILITIES WITH GREAT BRITAIN

Jackson had never fully recovered from his painful experiences with the British, the death of his brothers during the Revolutionary War, and his imprisonment by enemy troops. It was therefore no surprise that he was anxious to serve his country when Great Britain once again began threatening the United States. Still largely unwilling to accept the loss of control over their former North American colonies, the British had started to engage in hostilities that included capturing U.S. sailors and urging Indians to plot attacks against settlements in the states.

Such actions were ill received by many Americans, including Jackson, who were eager to see the nation expand southward into Spanish Florida and west into untamed areas beyond the frontier that were occupied by Indians. When the United States declared war on Great Britain in June 1812, Jackson was ready for action. Yet just as he had little experience when he first arrived in Philadelphia as a congressman, he had spent limited time on the battlefield before 1812.

Despite this fact, Jackson recognized that the war was the perfect occasion for an ambitious officer to advance both his military and political careers. As leader of the Tennessee state militia, Jackson had authority over approximately 2,500 men. He used his own money to supply his men with rifles and prepare them for service. He eagerly offered his military assistance to the government and waited to be called to duty.

That call came in December 1812, when Jackson was ordered to prepare his troops to march into New Orleans, Louisiana—a major port that could potentially decide the war if it fell under British control. Though the journey southward lasted more than a month and took place during the freezing winter, Jackson rallied his men onward and did everything in his power to keep their spirits up. After navigating the frosty Cumberland, Ohio, and Mississippi rivers, they at last arrived in Natchez, Mississippi, where they were instructed to wait until New Orleans could be reinforced with supplies.

Jackson's best attempts to encourage his troops and remind them of their patriotic responsibilities failed to prepare them for the blow of being commanded to return home by the U.S. government in March 1813. Having been informed that their services were no longer required, the men faced defeat without ever having engaged in combat. Hungry and exhausted, they had suffered through two months of bleak winter and insufficient supplies because they believed in their general and in their country. Jackson did his best to reassure his soldiers that they had not been wrong.

"It is my duty," he wrote to Rachel, "to act as a father to the sick and to the well and to stay with them until I march into Nashville." The endurance he displayed during the unfinished New Orleans campaign earned him the nickname Old Hickory—a

Jackson served in the War of 1812.

reference to a tree with an especially tough wood. Jackson again dipped into his personal funds to provide for the men as they began the long trek home. From comforting ailing soldiers to giving up his own horses so that the sick would not have to walk, he remained unshakable in his sense of duty to Tennessee's forces.

On his return to Nashville in the spring of 1813, Jackson was, according to one local newspaper, "the most beloved and esteemed of private citizens in western Tennessee.". That opinion would spread across the nation as the war progressed and the commander was repeatedly called to the defense of his country. Primarily a local figure at the start of the conflict, Jackson emerged from the war with a nationwide reputation.

Courageous Commander and War Hero

*J*ackson's time at the Hermitage in 1813 was short-lived. The War of 1812 raged on, and the military hero from Nashville was once again called to action in October 1813.

Though in the process of recovering from shoulder and arm wounds related to a recent duel, Jackson accepted the challenge when the government ordered him southward to battle Creek Indians in what is now the state of Alabama. Although the war was primarily between Great Britain and the United States, the British urged Spaniards in Florida and American Indians to rise up against U.S. citizens. For many tribes who continued to lose their land as America expanded south and west, Great Britain's promise to protect their territory in exchange for a wartime alliance was extremely attractive. In the late summer of 1813 a Creek chief named Red Eagle led an attack that ended with the death of 247 U.S. settlers at Fort Mims, on the eastern bank of the Alabama River.

Jackson, like many other Tennesseans, was furious when he heard about the assault. For men and women who had struggled to build a life on the frontier, Indian raids were a constant threat. Most pioneers were more concerned about survival and expansion than they were about Indians having their land taken from them as the United States developed and grew as a nation. In the autumn of 1813, U.S. citizens were also disturbed by the role Indians were playing in the War of 1812.

The massacre at Fort Mims angered many Americans.

As Jackson and the Tennessee militia marched toward Creek territory with additional military units from Mississippi and Georgia, they were aided by Cherokee Indians and those Creeks who did not agree with the Red Sticks. Not all Indians chose to ally themselves with Great Britain, and some sided with Jackson's forces in the hopes that the U.S. government would help them preserve their land, just as the British had promised the Red Sticks they would do. Old Hickory accepted their support, as he was in desperate need of the reinforcements.

Jackson's men once again lacked the necessary food and supplies for a long campaign, and some soldiers attempted to desert his command. Jackson refused to tolerate such disloyalty and made it known that anyone who tried to flee service would be tried and shot for his cowardly actions. His iron will and determination to win may have seemed harsh to a few of his troops, but it also earned their respect and ultimately helped them overcome the Creeks.

In March 1814 Jackson enjoyed a massive victory at the Battle of Horseshoe Bend on the Tallapoosa River in Alabama. Though he took measures to spare as many Creek women and children as possible, he showed little mercy to Red Stick warriors, and Red Eagle finally submitted. The following August the chief signed the Treaty of Fort Jackson, which obliged his tribe to give up 23 million acres of its land to the U.S. government. Both the Creeks and Great Britain had suffered a major defeat at Jackson's hands; he had clearly demonstrated that his leadership abilities were not to be underestimated.

Jackson and his troops defeating various Creeks in Alabama in early 1814.

CARING FOR A CREEK ORPHAN

Following a battle in 1813, Jackson came upon a Creek orphan named Lyncoya. Jackson found the small boy alongside his dead mother. Taking pity on him, the general sent Lyncoya home to the Hermitage; he became a member of the family and was educated alongside Andrew Junior.

Lyncoya died at a young age after catching a disease called tuberculosis in 1828. Several historians suspect that Rachel never fully recovered from the loss. Some believe his death may have added to the stress that led to her own that same year.

Protecting an Invaluable Port

Despite his success at Horseshoe Bend, Jackson spent little time relaxing afterward. British troops were still waging a difficult and aggressive assault on the United States, including in the U.S. capital itself, Washington, D.C. Enemy forces burned much of the city; they left the White House a smoldering ruin and local residents terrified.

Jackson—who had been appointed a major general in the U.S. Army in May 1814—went on the offensive against the British. He launched an attack on the Gulf port of Pensacola in Spanish-controlled Florida. Although the United States earnestly wanted to avoid conflict with Spain, it was widely known that the British had been using Florida to recruit and train their Indian allies. In defiance of direct orders from the secretary of war, James Monroe, Jackson captured Pensacola in November 1814. He then moved west to New Orleans and started taking steps to defend that port city against invasion.

While the British eyed New Orleans because of its valuable location along the Gulf of Mexico, U.S. forces had done little to secure the area by the time Jackson arrived in December 1814. He realized he needed to act swiftly and pledged that he would "drive [the country's] enemies into the sea or perish in the effort." Jackson took his promise seriously; he declared **martial law**, a system of law enforcement imposed by the military, usually during a crisis. The residents of New Orleans were expected to obey curfews and other rules that Jackson and his commanders set in place. The city was famous for its colorful mixture of cultures and its elegant parties; it was up to Jackson to ensure that it was also unreachable to enemy attackers.

Jackson did everything possible to create an unbeatable defense. His plans included blocking waterways leading into New Orleans and organizing a fighting force of men from all walks of life. In addition to official military troops, Jackson also worked with freed African Americans, Indians, Frenchmen, and even pirates who were committed to protecting the city. All in all, however, the force under his command still numbered only between 3,500 and 5,000 strong. His men were at an undeniable disadvantage when compared with the more than 8,000 professional soldiers headed by British general Edward Pakenham.

Such a vast difference in size failed to faze Jackson, who boldly ordered his troops to exchange fire with Pakenham's fleet when they sailed onto Lake Borgne in New Orleans on December 13, 1814. The British had gained access to the waterway by capturing American gunboats positioned there, and the fighting that followed lasted for several weeks. It was not always clear who had the upper hand in the combat, but both sides were fierce in their attacks and counterattacks.

Though Pakenham's men had received more organized and official training, the patriots under Jackson's authority were committed to defending their nation and their freedoms. They also knew the land they were fighting on well and were therefore able to ambush the enemy from various hiding spots in New Orleans's swampy bayous. Yet, American troops also had a powerful advantage in the leadership that Jackson provided. Fearless in the face of being severely outnumbered, he did not hesitate to join his forces on the battlefield and to rally them to fight even harder when the odds seemed stacked against them.

"Do not mind these rockets," he cheerfully advised his men of the spectacular **artillery** that had been used by the invaders to

Jackson rallying his men onward as he rides through enemy artillery fire during the Battle of New Orleans.

bring Washington, D.C, to its knees just a few months before. "They are mere toys to amuse children." Jackson's courage and self-confidence helped his troops gain a victory over the British at New Orleans on January 8, 1815. On that date the Americans engaged in one final, deadly skirmish that resulted in more than two thousand British casualties, Pakenham's death, and the scrambling retreat of any remaining enemy forces into Lake Borgne. After the Battle of New Orleans, U.S. soldiers listed less than one hundred men as dead, wounded, or missing.

Jackson's great victory in Louisiana came after the war had already technically been won. Two weeks earlier the United States and Great Britain had ended the conflict with the signing

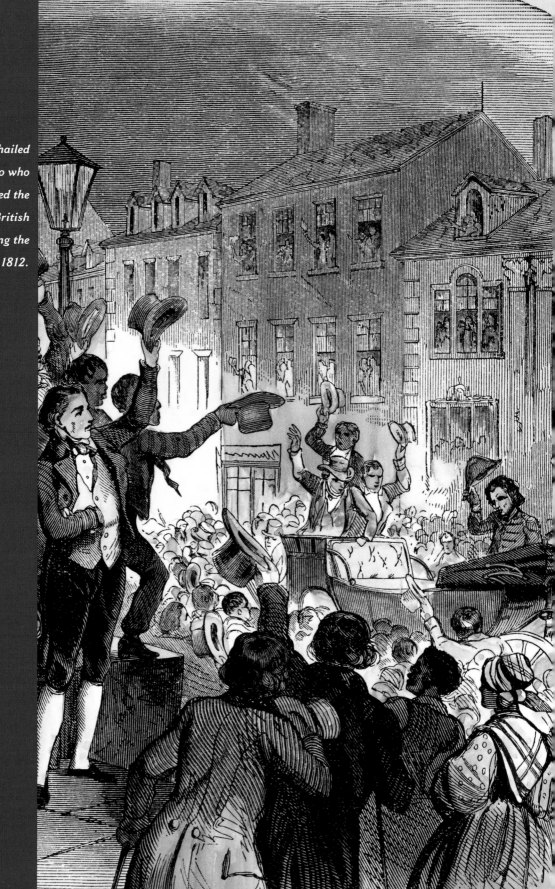

Jackson was hailed as a hero who had saved the country from British invasion during the war of 1812.

of the **Treaty of Ghent** in Belgium. During the nineteenth century, however, news spread slowly, especially when it was coming all the way from Europe. Even though Jackson's military success followed on the heels of U.S. officials' political discussions overseas, he was nonetheless hailed as a courageous and brilliant general. From New Orleans to Nashville throngs of grateful Americans celebrated his achievements and looked to Jackson as a national hero. He was even acclaimed in popular songs, including "The Eighth of January."

"Remember New Orleans I say,
Where Jackson [showed] them Yankee play,
And beat them off and [gained] the day,
And then we heard the people say
Huzza! For [General] Jackson."

REVISITING FLORIDA

Following the War of 1812 Jackson briefly returned to Rachel and the Hermitage after being named commander of the Army of the Southern District—the leader of all American military forces in the South. The few years' rest he enjoyed at home was greatly needed—forty eight years old and still suffering as a result of the many dueling wounds he had acquired over time, the war hero took great comfort in the company of his family and their farm. Yet, as he and Rachel had learned to expect, it was not long before duty called Jackson away once more.

"This is not a time for you to think of rest," President James Monroe wrote him in late 1817. "Great interests are at issue, and until our course is carried through triumphantly and every [form] of danger to which it is exposed is settled on the most solid foundation, you ought not to withdraw your active support from it." The great interests of which Monroe spoke centered around Florida, where Seminole Indians were stirring up trouble. This region, though owned by Spain, was considered valuable by most Americans. Controlling Florida would enable settlers to push farther southward, and it would also allow the United States to establish more ports along both the Atlantic Ocean and the Gulf of Mexico. However, the Seminoles, as well as the Spanish, stood in the way of winning the area.

The Seminoles of Florida, like so many other Indian tribes, were angry at the effects of U.S. expansion on territories held by their people. As a result, they were not about to give up their land without a fight and often became involved in skirmishes with settlers and U.S. soldiers along the Florida-Georgia and Florida-Alabama borders. President Monroe, responding to these hostilities, ordered Jackson to move south in early 1818 and force the tribe into submission. Though the president did not directly tell his commander to seize Florida from the Spanish, most historians agree that he hoped Jackson would indeed do just that.

Old Hickory did not disappoint government officials who secretly dreamed of winning the territory. As he marched through Florida with approximately three thousand U.S. troops and two thousand Indian allies, he took control of Spanish strongholds such as Saint Marks and Pensacola, which had fallen back into Spain's hands after the War of 1812. Along the way Jackson slaughtered countless Seminoles. He also executed two British subjects upon learning that they had been urging local Indians to attack U.S. settlers. This decision—along with his assault on Spanish forts—sparked outrage in Europe.

Some of Monroe's advisers wanted Jackson to be punished for his bold actions, which went far beyond any order to conquer the Seminoles and had set the United States on rather shaky ground with foreign powers. By 1819, however, most U.S. officials reluctantly agreed that any offense Old Hickory had given Great Britain and Spain was worthwhile. The Spanish, perhaps realizing how weak their grip on Florida actually was, agreed to sell the territory to the United States for $5 million.

Having at least temporarily quieted the Seminoles, Jackson gained national attention yet again. By the end of the Florida campaign, even his opponents admitted that he had played a major role in expanding the country. Some believed that he was now in a position to set his sights on the White House.

Jackson leading his troops in Pensacola in 1818.

Jackson sat for this portrait not long before he served as governor of Florida Territory.

Working a Way Toward the White House

$\mathcal{S}$ince Jackson had played such a major role in securing Florida for the United States, President Monroe decided to reward his star general with an offer of the governorship of the territory. Jackson accepted and, in the spring of 1821, departed with Rachel and a few of the young **wards** that the couple had taken in over the years. Though the family was sad to leave the Hermitage, Florida presented the potential for further political advancement and was not an opportunity to be refused.

The job that lay ahead of Jackson was not an easy one, however. Old Hickory had to work with Spanish officials who were clearly bitter about being forced to abandon their control of Florida. In addition, he quickly discovered that he did not have as much authority as he would have perhaps preferred from his seat in Pensacola, Florida. This state of affairs was largely due to the fact that Monroe and his advisers determined who would be appointed to government jobs in the territory.

Jackson found it difficult to establish new laws, a stable government, and an effective court system in Florida while struggling with the difficulties presented by the Spanish and even his own countrymen back in Washington, D.C. Nonetheless, he took his position as governor quite seriously, and he did accomplish these goals. He also established a series of important health codes aimed at the prevention of the deadly disease malaria; the area's hot, humid climate produced an abundance of mosquitoes—carriers of this disease.

A Fairly Large Family

Exactly how many children did Jackson and Rachel take under their care over the years? While they officially adopted two boys, the couple saw to the needs of about ten wards in the early 1800s. Sometimes these children had lost their father and continued to live with their mother at a location other than the Hermitage, but the Jacksons were considered their legal guardians. In this role, they were responsible for looking out for the youngsters' interests when it came to matters of money and education. As the years passed, many of the Jacksons' wards married and raised families of their own; several still lived or spent a great deal of time at the Hermitage during adulthood.

Despite Jackson's achievements in Florida, however, the territory did not appeal to the Tennessean. He and Rachel longed for Nashville and the Hermitage, especially after they themselves fell ill with malaria. Homesickness, poor health, and the overall challenges Jackson faced as governor drove him to resign from the post on December 1, 1821.

As happened so often after Jackson worked long and hard during a campaign in another part of the country, he was forced to spend several months physically recovering at the Hermitage. Weakened by his dueling wounds and the sickness he had suffered in Florida, he was grateful to have his wife see to his care while he rested and grew stronger. By then the

Jacksons were helping raise several children. As a result, they spent much of their time attending to family affairs and entertaining friends and relatives who frequently came to visit.

Though Rachel herself was not in the best of health, running the Hermitage with her husband seemed to make her happy. Those moments when Jackson was away were hard and lonely for her, and traveling with him to Florida had involved its own set of hardships. However, uninterrupted family life in Nashville never lasted long, either for her or for her ambitious husband. The presidential election of 1824 was only a few years away, and she and Jackson realized that Americans all over the country were eagerly hoping that Old Hickory would run for office.

The Most Popular Choice for President

From about 1800 to 1824 the **Democratic-Republican Party** was the main political party in the United States. Founded by James Madison and Thomas Jefferson, it supported states' rights and the idea of limited federal power. Party members also believed in strict construction, or strictly following the language of the **U.S. Constitution**. They worried that interpreting the wording of that document broadly would place too much power in the hands of federal politicians. Finally, Democratic-Republicans were committed to the welfare of America's farmers, laborers, and other average citizens rather than to the country's wealthy business and landowning classes.

This policy of being committed to the common man was one that Jackson considered particularly important. The men and women across the United States who knew about his commitment were anxious that he become a candidate in the presidential race of 1824. Jackson was not easily convinced that the job was right for him, though. He was a brilliant and bold military leader, but the battles he had fought in the South and on the western frontier were vastly different from the wars of words and complex debates that raged in Washington, D.C. Nevertheless, officials in Tennessee nominated him as early as 1822 to run in the election two years later. Jackson accepted and decided to resume his career on the national political scene in the meantime by agreeing to take a seat in the U.S. Senate in 1823.

Old Hickory believed himself to be a changed man by the time he arrived in the capital on December 3, 1823. No longer the hot-blooded youth of his early congressional years, he was calmer and more controlled and considered matters carefully before expressing his opinion. Wiser at fifty-six years old but just as determined to serve his country, Jackson had come to realize that the bold tactics he used to rally his men during military campaigns might not always work well on the Senate floor.

As statesman Sam Houston observed of him, "The general is calm, dignified, and makes as polished a bow as any man I have seen at court." But would Jackson's new manners in Congress be enough to triumph over the other three candidates who were aiming for the presidency in 1824? He was competing against Secretary of State John Quincy Adams, Secretary of the Treasury William H. Crawford, and Speaker of the U.S. House of Representatives Henry Clay. Each of these men had a great deal of political experience, but there was no denying that Old Hickory was a popular hero with the American people.

Like the men running against him, Jackson used songs, political cartoons, and newspaper articles during the course of his

Jackson was older and more dignified by the time he returned to the political scene in Washington, D.C., in 1823.

Jackson Forever!

The Hero of Two Wars and of Or'eans!

The Man of the People!

HE WHO COULD NOT BARTER NOR BARGAIN FOR THE

PRESIDENCY!

Who, although "*A Military Chieftain*," valued the purity of Elections and of the Electors, **MORE** than the Office of **PRESIDENT** itself! Although the greatest in the gift of his countrymen, and the highest in point of dignity of any in the world,

BECAUSE

It should be derived from the

PEOPLE!

No Gag Laws! No Black Cockades! No Reign of Terror! No Standing Army or Navy Officers, when under the pay of Government, to browbeat, or

KNOCK DOWN

Old Revolutionary Characters, or our Representatives while in the discharge of their duty. To the Polls then, and vote for those who will support

OLD HICKORY

AND THE ELECTORAL LAW.

A campaign poster for Jackson during the presidential election of 1824.

campaign. He swore that, if he was elected president, he would change the government so that it was more fair and just. When the public looked to Jackson, they remembered the patriot who fought bravely in the War of 1812, and they believed everything he promised.

The public was not the main consideration in presidential elections, however. A candidate needed to win a majority in the **electoral college**. Each state government chose a number of people, called electors, who voted in presidential races. As a rule, the electors selected the candidate who won the majority of the votes.

Though Jackson led in both popular and electoral tallies in late 1824, these successes did not guarantee him the White House. The public supported him with 151,271 votes, compared to the 113,122 they cast for Adams, who was the second favorite choice. In the electoral college Jackson's 99 votes to Adams's 84 were not enough to win. According to the Constitution, the victor needed the votes of more than 50 percent of the 260 electors. When no one had a majority, the House of Representatives decided who would become the president. Unfortunately for Jackson, Adams had more support in the House than he did.

"Rumors say that deep intrigue is on foot," Jackson wrote to acquaintances back in Tennessee. "That Mr. Clay is trying to wield his influence in favor of Adams." As Speaker of the House, Clay was in a position to persuade other representatives as they cast their votes. Would Old Hickory lose the election after having been the choice of the people?

This political cartoon dates back to 1824 and shows that year's presidential candidates in close competition for the White House.

John Quincy Adams was elected the sixth president of the United States.

Coping with Defeat and Corruption

Even though the way the U.S. government was set up in the late 1700s and early 1800s was designed to bring more justice and liberties to the people than they had experienced as British colonists, it was still not free from corruption. Political officials often made deals with one another to support certain issues or party members if doing so might advance their careers. In early 1825 Jackson's allies believed Clay had urged his fellow representatives to vote against Old Hickory.

When the House met on February 9, 1825, Jackson succeeded in gaining only seven votes. Adams, on the other hand, received thirteen—and won four years in the White House. When Adams promptly appointed Clay **secretary of state**, Jackson's supporters charged both men with making a corrupt bargain.

Old Hickory was furious at the final tally. While Jackson had initially doubted that he was the right man to lead the country, his campaign efforts and his obvious popularity with the people had convinced him otherwise. "Thus you see here," he wrote to a friend after Adams had been declared the victor, "the voice of the people . . . has been disregarded, and [political leaders] barter them as sheep . . . for their own views and personal [power]." Despite his outrage, however, Jackson congratulated the new president on his office. Old Hickory's conduct won him the admiration of many people, even those who had not voted for him.

Jackson was more determined than ever to overthrow Adams in the presidential race of 1828. Returning to the Hermitage, he immediately began working with a group of political allies that included Martin Van Buren and Vice President John C. Calhoun. Even members of Adams's own **cabinet** were disgusted by the rumors of corruption that tainted the 1824 election, and they advised Jackson that the moment might be right for him to break away from the Democratic-Republican Party, whose unity had been shattered by the contested race.

Resigning his Senate seat in the fall of 1825, Jackson used his time away from Congress to work with his supporters to shape what would ultimately become the Democratic Party. In October of that year, he was once again nominated to run for president and did not hesitate to accept. Still stinging from his recent loss in the House, he planned to use charges of corruption and unfair government practices to unseat Adams in 1828. Jackson also assured the people that he would provide them with leadership that would be devoted to their interests, instead of furthering the ambitions and wealth of a few privileged politicians. Many ordinary Americans, as well as several of Old Hickory's political colleagues, believed him.

Calhoun wrote Jackson a letter to this effect in June 1826, noting that his name "is found, as it always has been, on the side of liberty and your country." Yet Jackson's reputation and popularity did not guarantee an easy campaign that would be free from attacks on his character—and even on his beloved Rachel's.

TRIUMPH AMID TRAGEDY

*W*hile campaigning for the election of 1828, Jackson once again appeared to have the upper hand. This time, though, he could complain of the corruption and selfish interests that John Quincy Adams and Henry Clay had used to win control only four years before. Old Hickory promised to look out for the common man. He accused the current president and some of his officials of thinking only of themselves.

Although his supporters did the brunt of the work, Jackson still consulted them and was far from an absentee force during the campaign. He promised that, if he won the White House, he would fix the U.S. government; there would be no more secret deals or bargains between politicians at the expense of average Americans. He also took several other popular stands on issues of the day. For example, Jackson became famous for his opposition to the Bank of the United States (BUS). This institution had been founded during George Washington's presidency. **Chartered** by the U.S. government to regulate the nation's currency and money supply, the BUS influenced the conduct of banking across the nation. Yet Jackson was convinced that the country would be far better off without a central bank—partially because it had often been mismanaged and had been used for corrupt purposes.

During the campaign Jackson also expressed his views on westward expansion. He was clearly in favor of forcing various Indian tribes west of the Mississippi River to make way for

Americans who were eager to claim the land. Though his perspective would ultimately lead to disaster for millions of Indians, it was not surprising, given his desire to see the country grow and develop, as well as his frontier upbringing. Jackson had been raised on the edge of the wilderness, where the threat of attack by local tribes was always a danger. He sympathized with the interests of those like himself more than those of the Indians, whom he had spent a lifetime fighting.

Despite Old Hickory's popular ideas on improving the government and building the nation, the 1828 campaign was not an easy one for him. Adams and his supporters fought vigorously and made several attempts to ruin Jackson's reputation. Those who wanted to see the current president reelected reminded the public about Jackson's early days, fiery temper, and wild ways. They pointed to his youthful gambling, his drinking, and his reputation for dueling. Some even questioned his bravery at the famous Battle of New Orleans. All of these accusations were hard for Old Hickory to endure, but the bitterest insults he was forced to face involved rumors about his marriage to Rachel.

Adams's backers seized upon the opportunity to reveal the circumstances and timing of Rachel's separation from Robards, her first husband, and her subsequent union with Jackson. A few even mocked her physical appearance and personality (she was now older, plumper, and more serious than when she and Jackson had first met). The almost constant separation during his many military campaigns had taken an undeniable toll on Rachel's health. In addition, some of Adam's supporters took aim at the fact that she was clearly a simple country woman who lacked the elegance and graces of a Washington wife.

Do not be startled, gentle reader at the picture before you. It is all true and every body ought to know it. Gen. Jackson having made an assault upon Samuel Jackson, in the streets of Nashville, & the latter not being disposed to stand still and be beaten, stooped down for a stone to defend himself. While in the act of doing so, Gen. Jackson drew the sword from his cane and run it through Samuel Jackson's body, the sword entering his back and coming out of his breast. For this offence an indictment was found against Genl. Jackson, by a grand jury, upon which he was subsequently arraigned and tried. But finding means to persuade the petit jury that he committed the act in self-defence, he was acquitted. Gentle reader, it is for you to say, whether this man, who carries a sword cane, and is willing to run it through the body of any one who may presume to stand in his way, is a fit person to be our President.

A flyer published by Jackson's opponents in the election of 1828 criticise him for his supposed brutality as a general.

Combined with the death of her adopted son Lyncoya in June 1828, the taunts she bore at the hands of Jackson's attackers proved almost too much for Rachel. She cried constantly and dreaded the idea of leaving the Hermitage if her husband won the presidency. Jackson took great offense to any accusations involving his wife, but the circumstances of running in a national election left him few ways to defend her honor.

Rachel did not like the idea of serving as First Lady in Washington, D. C.

"I assure you," Rachel said of the events of 1828, "I had rather be a doorkeeper in the house of God than to live in that palace in Washington." Jackson's success with the people and his fellow politicians clearly did little to impress her or brighten her spirits. Yet, she could not have guessed how soon her wishes concerning "that palace in Washington" would be granted as the race for the White House drew to a close later that year.

The People's Own President

By the late fall of 1828, no one could deny that Jackson had won the majority of both popular and electoral votes. When the election concluded, 642,553 U.S. citizens had chosen him as their future president, along with 178 electors. In comparison, Adams received only 500,897 popular votes and 83 electoral votes.

Jackson was overjoyed at his success and at the thought of his upcoming move to Washington, D.C. Rachel was pleased to see her husband happy, but the victory itself and the idea of living in the public view distressed her. During the campaign she had experienced the pain of having false attacks made on her character. She realized that Jackson's win would only mean more of the same for her, and she secretly grieved at the prospect of leaving the shelter and familiarity of the Hermitage.

Sadness and stress continued to haunt Rachel; she ultimately suffered a fatal heart attack and died on December 22, 1828. The couple had been married thirty-eight years. The nation's new president had lost the person who meant more to him than anyone else. The overwhelmed Jackson blamed her death on the cruelty of his political enemies.

Despite his grief, however, Old Hickory had to focus on his duties. In late January 1829 he began his journey to Washington, DC, where he prepared to take office. His inauguration took place on March 4, and the day proved to be eventful.

The sun shone brightly following a cold, wet winter in the capital—weather conditions that one newspaper columnist for the *New York Evening Post* took as a sign that "nature was willing

TRIALS OF LIFE ALONE

Jackson vented his rage upon the men whom he believed had robbed him of his wife. He pointed his finger at the individuals who had attacked her character and appearance in the 1828 election. "I am left without her to encounter the trials of life alone," he declared to friends following her funeral. "I can forgive all those who have wronged me but will . . . have to pray that I may have grace to enable me to forget or forgive any enemy who has ever [hurt] that blessed one who is now safe from all suffering and sorrow, who they tried to put to shame for my sake."

to lend her aid towards contributing to the happiness of the thousands that crowded in to behold the great ceremony." Even if there had been pouring rain and freezing temperatures, though, the climate probably would not have been enough to keep the huge crowds away. Washington was packed with men and women of all backgrounds and walks of life who were eager to watch their new leader take office and make his way to the White House. Jackson was well aware of the people's presence, and he began his first presidential address by thanking them.

"Fellow-Citizens," he declared, "About to undertake the . . . duties that I have been appointed to perform by the choice of a free people, I [use] this customary and solemn occasion to express the gratitude [that] their confidence inspires." In his speech he promised to reduce the national debt, obey the U.S. Constitution, and uphold states' rights while still preserving the Union. Those who heard the words of the nearly sixty-two-year-old Jackson wildly displayed their enthusiasm, especially when he welcomed them to join him at the White House.

Following his invitation crowds of people crushed toward Old Hickory's new home. Never before had the executive mansion been so completely open to ordinary citizens, and some observers argued that it never should be again. Guests clumsily spilled food and liquor on the floor, and thousands of dollars worth of glass and china were shattered.

Fighting and chaos occasionally erupted as well. One Supreme Court judge who was known to oppose Jackson bitterly remarked, "The reign of King Mob seemed triumphant. I was glad to escape from the scene as soon as possible." Others viewed the events of Inauguration Day as proof of Old Hickory's deep love for Americans of all classes and backgrounds.

While traveling to Washington D.C., in 1829, Jackson sometimes stopped to deliver speeches to adoring crowds that gathered for a glimpse of their future president.

Swarms of people preparing to visit the White House after Jackson was sworn into office in 1829.

"It was a proud day for the people," the editors of a Kentucky newspaper called *The Argus of Western America* noted. "General Jackson is their own president." As the day ended on March 4, 1829, average Americans everywhere eagerly wondered how their nation would change and grow under "their own president" in the four years ahead.

Controversies with the Cabinet and Congress

Although greatly loved by the public for the most part, Jackson also had several enemies and political opponents. As is the case with most presidents, critics questioned his decisions from the very beginning of his term. Many of these men especially disagreed with Jackson about how appointments should be made to government offices.

In forming his cabinet the president selected individuals who had demonstrated their loyalty and support. For the important post of secretary of state, he chose Martin Van Buren, who became Jackson's vice president in his second term (John C. Calhoun was his first vice president). Yet, Jackson did not always seek advice on running the country from the heads of government departments. During his first term in office he began to rely upon the thoughts and opinions of personal friends and a handful of newspaper editors and journalists. This small group of informal advisers became known as the Kitchen Cabinet.

Jackson's early years as president were not free from controversy.

What further upset several politicians were Jackson's ideas about how long officials should be permitted to hold office. He believed that anyone appointed to a government position should step down every time a new president was elected. Jackson believed this practice would help end corruption because it would prevent individuals who were more interested in serving themselves than the people from remaining in control for too long.

A political cartoon mocking Jackson and his support of a spoils system.

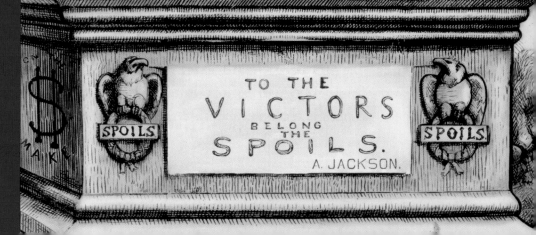

TO THE
VICTORS
BELONG
THE
SPOILS.
A. JACKSON.

SPOILS

SPOILS

In keeping with his views, Jackson fired almost 20 percent of the country's federal officials during his first eighteen months in office. Jackson's critics charged that his policies had less to do with the interests of average Americans than with his desire to reward his friends and supporters by granting them government posts.

This method of appointing and replacing government officials was controversial in its time and has remained so. Jackson's opponents called it the **spoils system** because he used it to give his supporters rewards, or spoils, in the form of government jobs. They emphasized that the new officeholders were appointed on the basis of whom they knew, rather than because of how qualified or experienced they were.

Rotation of office, as Jackson called it, was not the only immediate reform that unsettled Washington politicians. During his campaign, he had promised he would reduce the national debt. In Jackson's mind one way to battle corruption and lessen the amount of money America owed was to eliminate congressional waste, fraud, and abuse.

"Assure my friends," he wrote in 1829, "[that] we are getting on here well; we labor night and day and will continue to do so until we destroy all the rats who have been plundering the treasury." Jackson's reforms resulted in a savings of more than $51,000 his first year in office and the removal of several congressmen who were found guilty of misusing government funds. The president, however, also realized that he could not spend his entire term unseating and upsetting his fellow politicians. He understood that he needed Congress's support to achieve most of his presidential goals.

This portrait of Jackson was completed in 1830.

PROTECTING AND IMPROVING AMERICA *Seven*

When Jackson entered the White House, he already had many opponents, but his fellow Southerners confidently regarded him as a friend and ally. His vice president, John C. Calhoun, was from South Carolina, and Jackson himself supported various measures that benefited southern states. In addition, his policy of

removing the southeastern Indian tribes and relocating them across the Mississippi River met with widespread approval, especially in Georgia and Alabama, where citizens desired the use of the Indians' territory.

Jackson generally opposed legislation that benefited the North and and West and any individual states. For example, he vetoed the Maysville Road Bill on May 27, 1830. This bill involved setting aside money for the construction of a road between Maysville and Lexington, Kentucky. Jackson believed that a Kentucky road

John C. Calhoun served as Jackson's first vice president.

was the responsibility of Kentuckians. His reasoning was that federal government projects should aid the whole country, not merely certain individual states.

However, Jackson and many Southerners were at odds on one particular issue. Southern officials and congressmen, as well as Vice President Calhoun, opposed a **tariff**—a tax on imported goods—that Congress had passed in 1828. Since southern planters (and the South as a whole) depended upon the overseas trade in cotton and other farm products for their survival, they called this tariff, which would severely harm their economy, the Tariff of Abominations.

Vice President Calhoun, who led the opposition to the tariff, insisted that individual states had the right to **nullify** federal laws, or declare them invalid. Nullification would allow lawmakers from any part of the country to ignore any government rules they did not like. Jackson saw his vice president's ideas as a threat to the Union. States, he argued, were required to obey the laws of the federal government. In Calhoun's opinion, though, such obedience was not necessarily a good thing. He believed that states even had the right to **secede** or withdraw, from the Union if they so chose.

Some Southerners may have expected Jackson to back them up, but they were proved wrong. Though he claimed to favor states' rights, his many years of service in the military seemed to have encouraged him to think from a national perspective. The several battles Old Hickory had fought were on behalf of the United States of America, not individual states or regions. While he supported a handful of policies that Southerners favored, he was more devoted to the overall welfare of the country as a whole. Jackson made his opinions clear at a dinner party in the spring of 1830, following a discussion in which Calhoun defended states' rights.

"Our Union," remarked the president as he proposed a toast, "it must be preserved." Everyone present noticed that Jackson was looking at Calhoun as he spoke. In returning the toast, Calhoun responded, "The Union, next to our liberty, most dear."

Tensions between Calhoun and Jackson continued to grow. Calhoun resigned the vice presidency in 1832 to return to the Senate. Although the nullification crisis lost some of its urgency, talk of secession remained throughout Jackson's presidency. Both Old Hickory and his former vice president were determined to stand up for what they believed was best for the country.

A Tragic Move for American Indians

Some of what Jackson believed brought hardship, pain, and death to countless Indians. Tribes who lived east of the Mississippi River—particularly in the states of Georgia, Mississippi, Alabama, and Florida—resided on fertile and mineral-rich land, land that Americans and their government officials were eager to claim for themselves. Everyone from farmers to businessmen was interested in these areas. For the Choctaw, Chickasaw, Creek, Seminole, Cherokee, and other Indians, however, giving up or selling their territory to benefit their American neighbors had little appeal.

The Indian nations had struggled for two centuries against first Europeans and then Americans who wanted them to either **assimilate** or, more often, abandon their lands. They had no ally in Jackson. Like many others who had grown up on the frontier, he viewed Indians as the enemy. In addition, he had battled several tribes during the War of 1812 and his Florida campaigns. He sided with those who wanted the southeastern tribes moved farther west, by force if necessary.

In 1830, Jackson was sixty-three years old and in the second year of his presidency and still had an urge to push the frontier westward. To strengthen and expand the United States, he had already battled Great Britain and Spain. He was not ready to allow the Indian nations to stand in the way of what he saw as his country's destiny.

Jackson therefore signed the Indian Removal Act on May 26, 1830. This bill gave the president the power to move all Indians dwelling east of the Mississippi River west of that waterway. Congress appropriated $5,000,000 to pay for the lands belonging to the Cherokee Indians, some of whom were willing to be resettled peacefully. Certain Choctaw Indians were permitted to remain east of the Mississippi, but they had to agree to accept U.S. citizenship, obey American laws, and give up all claims to their ancestral territories.

While most Americans in the South supported Jackson's policy of Indian removal, which allowed them to acquire valuable land, people in the Northeast and Midwest were less enthusiastic. Though some of them believed the president was treating the Indians unfairly, Jackson remained unmoved by any opposition.

"Our children by thousands yearly leave the land of their birth to seek new homes in distant regions," Jackson declared to Congress in 1830. "Can it be cruel in this government when, by events which it cannot control, the Indian is made discontented in his ancient home to purchase his lands, to give him a new and

An Enormous Evil

One Massachusetts congressman, Edward Everett, warned Jackson that his decision to support the Indian Removal Act would have tragic consequences. "The evil . . . is enormous," he noted. "The inevitable suffering [is] incalculable. Do not stain the fair fame of the country. . . . Nations of dependent Indians, against their will, under color of law, are driven from their homes into the wilderness. You cannot explain it; you cannot reason it away. . . . Our friends will view this measure with sorrow, and our enemies alone with joy. And we ourselves . . . shall look back upon it, I fear, with self-reproach and a regret as bitter as unavailing."

extensive territory, to pay the expense of his removal, and support him a year in his new abode? How many thousands of our own people would gladly embrace the opportunity of removing to the West on such conditions! If the offers made to the Indians were extended to them, they would be hailed with gratitude and joy."

Few Indians, however, felt gratitude and joy as they headed westward. The Cherokees in particular were forced to endure a heartbreaking 1,200-mile journey that took them from Georgia to new territories on the other side of the Mississippi River. About four thousand Indians died from starvation and sickness along the way. The horrific experience they endured has become known as the Trail of Tears.

Jackson could not have known at the time that his support of the Indian Removal Act would be remembered more for the Cherokees' suffering than for his success in expanding U.S. territory. Indian removal was, however, only one of many of his policies that affected America's future. Jackson's approach to foreign affairs and the national bank also shaped the nation's course.

Jackson is still remembered for his role in the Trail of Tears.

Creating Diplomacy and Undoing the Bank

When Jackson became president, the United States was still struggling to repay its national debt and gain the respect of other countries. During his first term in office he signed a trade agreement with Great Britain involving the shipment of goods to and from the West Indies, a string of commercially important islands in the Caribbean Sea.

He also struck an agreement with the government of France. During Europe's Napoleonic Wars (1803–1815), in which the French and British battled one another, French warships stopped U.S. trading vessels that were suspected of carrying cargo bound for Great Britain and seized their goods. Americans who owned the merchandise had long been demanding compensation for the thefts. Jackson put pressure on the French to repay these U.S. citizens. The two nations came to terms in 1831, but it took the French government a few more years to actually begin repayment.

Jackson's administration also conducted **diplomacy** with many other world powers besides France. Jackson worked to create relationships with countries in Asia, South America, and various parts of Europe. As the election of 1832 drew nearer, his diplomatic successes raised his stature among voters, many of whom took pride in the impressive position of the United States as an independent nation. In addition, the money that poured in from around the globe because of the favorable trade agreements that Jackson had negotiated greatly reduced the national debt.

Yet not all of the president's policies met with approval. Representative Henry Clay, who planned on running against Jackson in 1832, clashed with the president on the topic of the

Jackson meeting with statesmen in the White House, where he served another four years after the 1832 presidential elections.

Bank of the United States (BUS). The first BUS had been created by individuals who believed that it was wise to give the government an important role in the monetary and financial aspects of the nation's economy. The bank's supporters argued that it allowed government officials to work hand in hand with big businesses for the nation's good.

The bank's **charter** (its authorization to do business) was up for congressional renewal in 1832, but Jackson was convinced that the institution had outlived its usefulness. He declared that the BUS was a form of government corruption that hurt average Americans. A few officials and wealthy businessmen used the bank to control the economy to their own benefit but to the harm

A political cartoon that depicts Jackson overshadowing supporters of the BUS who had hoped to see that institution's charter renewed in 1832.

of the farmers and small business owners who made up the bulk of the country's population. Jackson thought that getting rid of the national bank would permit investors and less powerful regional financial institutions to come to arrangements better suited to their needs.

Henry Clay and other members of Congress who favored the BUS became involved in a heated debate with Jackson that called the Bank War. Renewal of the bank's charter was a major issue in the 1832 election campaign. In July 1832, after Congress approved a bill that renewed the charter, Jackson vetoed it.

"The bank," he told Martin Van Buren, "is trying to kill me, but I will kill it!" In this struggle, as in many others, Jackson ultimately triumphed. In the meantime, however, he had to face Clay and two lesser-known candidates, John Floyd and William Wirt, in an election that would decide whether the people would grant him another four years in the White House.

FINAL YEARS OF THE PIONEER PRESIDENT

Eight

$\mathcal{D}$uring the election of 1832 Jackson's principal opponent was Henry Clay. There had been poor relations between them since 1825, when Clay helped John Quincy Adams win the presidency. The intervening years had seen the formation of new political alliances, and in the 1832 election the candidates appeared under the banners of new parties. Old Hickory ran as a Democrat, and Clay was the choice of the National Republicans. Because of his decisive break with John C. Calhoun, Jackson chose Martin Van Buren of New York as his vice-presidential running mate.

Though his political opponents mockingly referred to Jackson as King Andrew—a tyrant who was more interested in ruling than serving the country—a majority of voters and members of the electoral college disagreed. Jackson won a decisive victory in the 1832 election. The sixty-five-year-old general was still the people's choice, and even his opponent William Wirt noted his astounding popularity. "My opinion," observed Wirt, "is that [Jackson] may be president for life if he

This political cartoon shows Jackson in a monarch's robes—dressed as "King Jackson."

chooses." Once the election was over, however, Jackson still had to face those politicians who opposed him on various issues of the day. Besides the renewal of the BUS's charter, disputes over states' rights, nullification, and secession also created controversy. In the wake of his electoral victory Jackson was less disposed to compromise than ever before. In many of his battles with Congress as a whole and with representatives of individual states, he often proved the victor.

By 1836 it was clear that the expired bank charter would never again be renewed. In addition, South Carolina congressmen—who had kept the issues of nullification and secession alive during the first part of Jackson's second term—agreed for a time to accept most federal laws and remain within the Union. Though he was sixty-nine and in declining health as his presidency drew to a close, Old Hickory could look upon the previous eight years as a period when he won more fights than he lost. When he left office, many average citizens considered him a hero.

According to Amos Kendall, an official who worked closely with Jackson, "His reelection . . . [was] deemed by us essential to the interests of our country, if not to the existence of the Union." One of Jackson's final presidential acts was to have far-reaching effects.

RECOGNIZING TEXAS AND RETURNING TO TENNESSEE

Since the early 1820s growing numbers of U.S. citizens had been moving to Texas, a huge area in the southwest belonged to the neighboring nation of Mexico. Many of these settlers were in favor of **annexing** Texas to the United States—that is, making the vast territory a part of their home country. Mexican officials refused to sell the land when Jackson made offers to buy it from

A battle at a fortress called the Alamo during the Texas Revolution.

them during his first term. By 1835 their stubbornness and American residents' desire to gain independence from foreign control sparked an uprising known as the Texas Revolution (1835–1836). General Samuel Houston successfully led the settlers to victory. In 1836 Houston and other Texans turned to Jackson and Congress and asked that Texas be annexed.

Jackson, however, was concerned that annexation would upset northern politicians, who were largely opposed to adding any territory to the Union where slavery might take root. The nation was growing ever more divided over whether the ownership of African-American slaves should be permitted. Many in the South supported slavery, but a majority in the North was against it. Each side was interested in limiting the political influence of the other and saw the annexation of Texas as something that could permanently alter the balance of sectional power.

Jackson also realised, though, that expansion was another important issue at stake. The annexation of Texas would be a major step in broadening U.S. borders. Because of the strength of the opposition, however, Jackson could not take this step. Instead, as he prepared to leave office in March 1837, he formally recognized Texas's independence from Mexico.

Texas would not officially be added to the Union until 1845. Jackson's decision to get the process started by acknowledging Texan's freedom and sending a diplomatic representative there paved the path for things to come—things that included a bloody war with Mexico (1846–1848).

Jackson was long gone from the White House before either Texas statehood or the Mexican War arrived. In November 1836 Martin Van Buren, Jackson's vice president and chosen successor, was elected president. The following winter, Old Hickory packed his belongings to return to the Hermitage. Just as he had been warmly welcomed by crowds on the day of his inauguration eight years earlier, people from all walks of life gathered to bid Jackson a fond farewell.

As his train departed for Tennessee, an observer remarked that it was "as if a bright star had gone out of the sky." Jackson might have stepped away from directing the government, but he kept busy during his retirement. Several of the wards he and Rachel had taken in over the years lived in Tennessee, and he saw them often. In addition, he stayed aware of current political issues and spent a great deal of time and money restoring the plantation and tending to day-to-day responsibilities at the Hermitage.

Like many other southern plantation owners, Jackson kept slaves to work the land and care for the property. Many Americans—both Northerners and Southerners—considered slavery cruel and opposed to everything the nation stood for. Nevertheless, large-scale agricultural production in the South depended on the availability of forced labor to produce the great

Jackson during his retirement at the Hermitage.

amounts of cotton, tobacco, and other crops that were an important part of the national economy. Whether Jackson or not realized it, the issue of slavery would rip apart the Union he had fought hard to preserve with the onset of the Civil War (1861–1865). Yet Old Hickory did not live long enough to witness the bloody division of the nation he had proudly led.

THE LAST GLIMMER

Jackson was not a man to let poor health stop him from serving his country. He had led charges on the battlefield and dealt with national crises from the capital while suffering from dueling wounds or illnesses that caused him to cough up blood. When Rachel was alive, she had nursed him if he was unwell, and when he was a soldier, he had been able to return to the Hermitage between military campaigns. His many physical complaints finally began to catch up with him in the 1840s.

The general who was nicknamed for being as tough as wood was forced to admit, "My lamp is nearly burned out, and the last glimmer has come." By 1845 Jackson was nearly blind, had almost constant trouble breathing, and often struggled with chills and fever. He was seventy-eight years old when death came to him at the Hermitage on June 8, 1845. Shortly before he passed away, he requested that he be buried without any great ceremony, ordered his loved ones to be good and obedient children, and further instructed that they not grieve for him. He was laid to rest beside Rachel on the grounds of the Hermitage.

Besides his estate in Tennessee, though, what legacy did Old Hickory leave behind? Years after his death, one of his former slaves, a man named Alfred, was asked if he believed Jackson would get into heaven. "If [General] Jackson takes it into his head to [get] to heaven," Alfred replied, "who's [going] to keep him out?"

The man whom Alfred described had built a reputation for bravery and for devotion to his country. These personal qualities helped him win many of the fights he fought, whether he was dueling in Kentucky, battling in the swamps of New Orleans, or

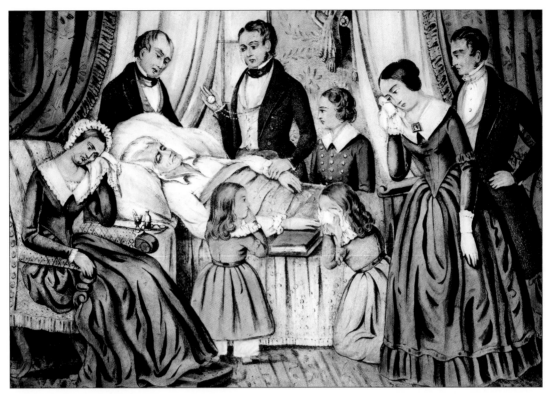

Jackson surrounded by his loved ones at his deathbed.

speaking his mind in a government meeting hall. No matter where he was fighting, Old Hickory put forth all his efforts on behalf of what he held dear, which included his beloved Rachel's honor, the strength of the Union, and the interests and freedoms of ordinary men and women. Sometimes his enemies accused him of being common; sometimes they complained that he acted like a king. Regardless of the controversies his decisions sparked or of the politicians he angered, Jackson, a man who blended a pioneer's spirit with a soldier's honor, was driven by a sense of patriotism that guided all his actions, from his days in the Waxhaws to his years in the White House.

As he stated in 1837 during his farewell address in Washington, D.C, "My public life has been a long one, and I cannot hope that it has at all times been free from errors; but I have the [comfort] of knowing that, if mistakes have been committed, they have not seriously injured the country I so anxiously [tried] to serve, and, at the moment when I surrender my last public trust, I leave this great people prosperous and happy, in the full enjoyment of liberty and peace, and honored and respected by every nation of the world. . . . I thank God that my life has been spent in a land of liberty and that He has given me a heart to love my country with the affection of a son." More than a century and a half after Jackson's death, his legacy, however much it may be debated, lives on in Tennessee, in the nation's capital, and in the very soil of the America he loved.

OLD HICKORY'S STYLE OF DEMOCRACY

Jackson's contributions to the Democratic Party and to the nation as a whole were so important that his political beliefs and practices are often referred to as Jacksonian Democracy. This concept is defined by commitment to the interests of ordinary men and women and to the territorial expansion of the nation. It also includes a desire to strengthen the powers of the president—and to limit those of Congress.

Jackson's legacy as a national leader lives on in the twenty-first century.

1767

Born (March 15) in the Waxhaws region of the Carolinas

1780

Fights for the patriot cause
during the Revolutionary War

1788

Serves as solicitor general
for the western district of
North Carolina

1791

Marries Rachel Donelson

1796

Becomes a U.S. congress-
man from Tennessee and
serves in the House of
Representatives.

1797

Is appointed a U.S. senator
from Tennessee

1802

Is elected a major general of
the Tennessee militia

1814

Is appointed a major general
of the U.S. Army

1700

1821
Is named governor of the territory of Florida

1825
Loses the 1824 presidential election when the House of Representatives votes for John Quincy Adams

1828
Is elected the seventh president of the United States

1832
Wins reelection to the presidency

1837
Leaves office and returns to his Tennessee home, the Hermitage

1845
Dies at the Hermitage at the age of seventy-eight

1850

NOTES

CHAPTER ONE

p.10, ". . . throw him three times out of four . . .": boyhood acquaintance of Jackson. "Exclusive Amazon.com Q&A with Jon Meacham and H. W. Brands," 16 Nov. 2008 ("American Lion: Andrew Jackson in the White House," *Bookmarks Magazine*, 12. Feb. 2009), www.bookmarksmagazine.com/book-review/american-lion-andrew-jackson-white-house/jon-meacham/.

p.14, ". . . are popping them still . . . ": Andrew Jackson, "The War in the Carolinas," *The Life of Andrew Jackson*, James Parton (Boston: Houghton, Osgood, 1879), p. 74.

p.15, ". . . not quite six feet long and a little over . . .": Andrew Jackson, "Childhood and Youth," *History of Andrew Jackson—Pioneer, Patriot, Soldier, Politician, President*, Augustus C. Buell (New York: Scribner, 1904), p. 2.

p.15, ". . . last words to me when about to start for Charleston . . .": Andrew Jackson, "Childhood and Youth," *History of Andrew Jackson—Pioneer, Patriot, Soldier, Politician, Presideny* Buell, p. 57.

CHAPTER TWO

p.17, ". . . roaring, rollicking . . . horse-racing, card-playing, mischievous . . .": Waxhaws local, "A Roaring Fellow," *Andrew Jackson*, Sean Wilentz (New York: Times Books, 2005), p. 18.

p.19, "quite a beau in the town": lady from Salisbury, "Boy from the Waxhaw District," *The Life of Andrew Jackson*, Robert V. Remini (New York: HarperCollins, 2001; first published 1988), p. 10.

p.20, ". . . the Jackson that used to live in Salisbury . . .": Salisbury townswoman, "Boy from the Waxhaw District," *The Life of Andrew Jackson*, Remini, p. 10.

p.21, ". . . and feelings are injured, he ought . . ." Andrew Jackson, "Frontiersman and Lawyer," *The Life of Andrew Jackson*, Remini, pp. 14–15.

p.23, "She was irresistible to men": relative (first quoted) of Rachel Donelson, "A Life on His Own," *The Generals—Andrew Jackson, Sir Edward Pakenham, and the Road to the Battle of New Orleans*. Benton Rain Patterson (New York: New York University Press, 2005), p. 19.

p.23, ". . . the best dancer, the sprightliest companion . . ." relative (second quoted) of Rachel Donelson, "A Life on His Own," *The Generals—Andrew Jackson, Sir Edward Pakenham, and the Road to the Battle of New Orleans*. Patterson, p. 19.

p.25, ". . . will not be heaven to me if I do not . . .": Andrew Jackson, p. 388. "Religion—Last Days," *The True Andrew Jackson*, Cyrus Townsend Brady (Philadelphia: Lippincott, 1906), p. 388.

CHAPTER THREE

p.27, ". . . with long locks of hair hanging over his face . . .": Albert Gallatin, "Congress-man Jackson," *The Life of Andrew Jackson*, Remini, p. 35.

p.29, ". . . wretched state is very fitly . . .": visitor to the U.S. capitol during Jackson's early days as a congressman, *Life on the Circuit with Lincoln*, p. 526 (Northern Illinois University Libraries Digitalization Projects, 12 Feb. 2009), http://lincoln.lib.niu.edu/cgi-bin/philologic/getobject.pl?p.3612:526.lincoln (date last updated not available).

p.30, ". . . passions are terrible. He could never speak . . .": Thomas Jefferson, "Web-ster's Descriptions," *The Life of Thomas Jefferson*, Henry S. Randall (New York: Derby and Jackson, 1858), p. 506.

p.32, ". . . no great service you have rendered the country . . .": John Sevier, "A Fighting District Attorney," *The Life of Andrew Jackson*, Parton, p. 164.

p.33, "Oh! I believe that he has . . .": Andrew Jackson, "The Duel," *The Life of Andrew Jackson*, Parton, p. 300.

p.37, ". . . to act as a father to the sick and to the well . . ." Andrew Jackson, "Old Hickory," *The Life of Andrew Jackson*, Remini, p. 300.

p.38, ". . . most beloved and esteemed of private citizens . . .": Nashville newspaper editorial, *The Life of Andrew Jackson*, Remini, p. 300.

CHAPTER FOUR

p.43, "drive [the country's] enemies into to sea or perish . . .": Andrew Jackson, "New Orleans," *The Battle of New Orleans*, Robert V. Remini. (New York: Penguin, 2001, first published 1999), p. 43.

p.44, ". . . not mind these rockets . . .": Andrew Jackson, "New Orleans," *The Battle of New Orleans*, Remini, p. 99.

p.47, "Remember New Orleans when I say . . .": "The Eighth of January," *Winning the Battle of New Orleans—January 8, 1815* (The Library of Congress—America's Story from America's Library, 12 Feb. 2009), www.americaslibrary.gov/cgi-bin/page.cgi/jb/nation/jackson_3 (date last updated not available).

p.47, ". . . interests are at issue, and until . . .": James Monroe, "Florida," *The Life of Andrew Jackson*, Remini, p. 86.

CHAPTER FIVE

p.54, ". . . general is calm, dignified, and makes as polished . . ." Sam Houston, "Return to the Senate," *Andrew Jackson and the Course of American Freedom (1822–1832)*, Robert V. Remini. (New York: Harper and Row, 1981), p. 60.

★ ★ ★ ★ ★ ★ ★ ★ ★ ★ ★ ★ ★ ★ ★ ★ ★

p.57, ". . . say that deep intrigue . . .": Andrew Jackson, "The Theft of the Presidency," *Andrew Jackson and the Course of American Freedom (1822–1832),* Remini, p. 85.

p.59, ". . . the voice of the people has been disregarded.": Andrew Jackson, "The Theft of the Presidency," *Andrew Jackson and the Course of American Freedom (1822–1832),* Remini, p. 96.

p.60, ". . . is found, as it always has been.": John C. Calhoun, "Organizing an Opposition," *Andrew Jackson and the Course of American Freedom (1822–1832),* Remini, pp. 112–113.

Chapter Six

p.64, ". . . rather be a doorkeeper in the house of God . . .": Rachel Jackson, ". . . Such Expectations . . . ," *First Ladies: The Saga of the Presidents' Wives and Their Power (1789–1961),* Carl Sferrazza Anthony (New York, HarperCollins, 1990), p. 112.

p.65, ". . . left without her to encounter the trials of life . . .": Andrew Jackson, "Triumph and Tragedy," *Andrew Jackson and the Course of American Freedom (1822–1832),* Remini, p. 154.

p.66, ". . . willing to lend her aid towards contributing to the happiness of the thousands . . ." *New York Evening Post*<1> columnist, "The First People's Inaugural," *Andrew Jackson and the Course of American Freedom (1822–1832),* Remini, p. 173.

p.66, ". . . duties that I have been appointed to perform . . .": *Andrew Jackson, First Inaugural Address of Andrew Jackson* (Yale Law School—The Avalon Project. 12 Feb. 2009), http://avalon.law.yale.edu/19th_century/jackson1.asp (date last updated not available).

p.66, ". . . reign of King Mob seemed . . .": Supreme Court judge, Chapter 73, Jackson — "Liberty and Union, Now and Forever"—Van Buren—Hard Times. 31 Aug. 2004 (The University of Pennsylvania—A Celebration of Women Writers. 12 Feb. 2009), http://digital.library.upenn.edu/women/marshall/country/country-VII-73.html.

p.68, ". . . a proud day for the people . . .": editors at *The Argus of Western America,* The Rise of Jacksonian Democracy—Eyewitness Accounts, 2006 (The White House Historical Association. 12 Feb. 2009), www.whitehousehistory.org/04/subs/04_b_1828.html> (specific date last updated not available).

p.71, ". . . we are getting on here well . . .": "The Reform Begins," *Andrew Jackson and the Course of American Freedom (1822–1832),* Remini, p. 87.

CHAPTER SEVEN

p.75, ". . . It must be preserved.": Andrew Jackson, *Jacksonian Democracy* (The University of Houston—Digital History, 12 Feb. 2009), www.digitalhistory.uh.edu/database/article_display.cfm?HHID=639.

p.75, ". . . next to our liberty most dear.": John C. Calhoun, *Jacksonian Democracy* (The University of Houston—Digital History, 12 Feb. 2009), www.digitalhistory.uh.edu/database/article_display.cfm?HHID=639.

p.76, ". . . inevitable suffering [is] incalculable . . .": Edward Everett, *Speeches on the Passage of the Bill for the Removal of the Indians Delivered in the Congress of the United States* (Statements from the Debate on Indian Removal, Columbia University. 12 Feb. 2009), www.columbia.edu/~lmg21/BC3180/removal.html; http://cherokeehistory.com/picture.html (specific date last updated not available).

p.76, ". . . yearly leave the land of their birth to seek new homes in . . .": Andrew Jackson, "President Andrew Jackson's Case for the Removal Act," First Annual Message to Congress, 8 December 1830. 30 Jan. 2009 (Mount Holyoke College: International Relations Program, 12 Feb. 2009), www.mtholyoke.edu/acad/intrel/andrew.htm.

p.81, ". . . is trying to kill me, but I will kill . . .": Andrew Jackson, "Andrew Jackson—1829–1837" (About the White House—Presidents, 12 Feb. 2009), www.whitehouse.gov/about/presidents/andrewjackson/ (date last updated not available).

CHAPTER EIGHT

p.83, ". . . may be president for life if he chooses . . .": William Wirt, "Jackson, the Union, and Democracy,"*Andrew Jackson and the Course of American Freedom (1822–1832),* Remini, p. 392.

p.84, ". . . deemed by us essential to the interests of our . . .": Amos Kendall, "Jackson, the Union, and Democracy," *Andrew Jackson and the Course of American Freedom (1822–1832),* Remini, p. 391.

p.86, ". . . a bright star had gone out . . .": Observer who witnessed Jackson's departure from Washington, D.C., in 1837, "Faces from the Past—V," 2008 (*American Heritage Magazine,* 12 Feb. 2009), www.americanheritage.com/articles/magazine/ah/1961/1/1961_1_16.shtml (specific date last updated not available).

p.75, ". . . is nearly burned out, and the last glimmer . . .": Andrew Jackson, "Faces from the Past—V," 2008 (*American Heritage Magazine.* 12 Feb. 2009), www.americanheritage.com/articles/magazine/ah/1961/1/1961_1_16.shtml (specific date last updated not available).

p.88, ". . . takes it into his head to . . .": Alfred (one of Jackson's slaves), "Faces from the Past—V," 2008 (*American Heritage Magazine*. 12 Feb. 2009), www.americanheritage.com/articles/magazine/ah/1961/1/1961_1_16.shtml (specific date last updated not available).

p.90, ". . . cannot hope that it has at all times . . .": Andrew Jackson, Farewell Address (March 4, 1837) (The Miller Center of Public Affairs at the University of Virginia—American President: Andrew Jackson, 12 Feb. 2009), http://millercenter.org/scripps/archive/speeches/detail/3644 (date last updated not available).

GLOSSARY

annex in a political context, to incorporate a territory into a country or join one territory to another

artillery large, transportable weapons of war, including rockets and cannons; also, the branch of the armed forces that uses such weapons

assimilate to become similar to individuals who are part of a larger or more mainstream social group.

cabinet that official advisory body to a president or another head of state. Cabinet members head various government departments

charter contract or other binding legal mechanism that establishes an institution, such as a bank or a corporation, whose obligations, rights, and sphere of activity are defined.

delegate in American political history, a territory's representative in Congress. A territorial delegate could speak on the territory's behalf but could not cast a vote.

Democratic Party the major political party in the United States from the mid–1820s to the 1860; since then, one of the two major political parties (the other being the Republican Party). Before the Civil War the party generally favored states' rights, tax and tariff legislation that did not benefit one region at the expense of another, westward expansion of the nation, and a stronger presidency. The party attempted to remain neutral on the contentious issue of slavery.

Democratic-Republican Party the main political party in the United States from about 1800 to 1824; the party favored states' rights, limitations on the scope of federal power, a strict interpretation of the language of the U.S. Constitution, and the extension of the right to vote.

★ ★ ★ ★ ★ ★ ★ ★ ★ ★ ★ ★ ★ ★ ★ ★ ★

diplomacy the skills connected with the delicate process of establishing and maintaining peaceful relationships between nations.

electoral college in U.S. political races, the assembled electors of each state, who, acting in accord with the results of the state's balloting, cast their votes (normally on a winner-take-all basis) to choose the president.

House of Representatives one of the two legislative bodies, or houses, that make up the U.S. Congress, the other being the Senate. The number of each state's representatives—there are 435 representatives in all—is proportional to its population.

Loyalist during the Revolutionary era, an American colonist who remained loyal to Great Britain (often also called a Tory).

martial law a system of law enforcement imposed or administered by military forces, especially during times of crisis.

militia a force of able-bodied men (and sometimes women), recruited from the ranks of ordinary citizens, who provide for the safety of persons and property along with or in the absence of regular military forces.

nullify in American history, for an individual state or states to declare that a law enacted by the federal government is null and void.

secede to leave or withdraw from a group or an affiliation. In American history *secession* refers to a state's withdrawal from the Union established by the U.S. Constitution.

secretary of state the member of the U.S. president's cabinet who oversees foreign relations. The Department of State was the first executive-branch department to be established.

solicitor general a law officer employed by a government who performs legal work for that government.

spoils system a system of patronage in which elected officials made appointments on the basis of party loyalty and support instead of merit or ability.

tariff a tax on imported goods.

Tory another term for a Loyalist during the Revolutionary era.

Treaty of Ghent the treaty, signed on December 24, 1814, that officially ended the War of 1812 and restored peaceful relations between the United States and Great Britain.

U.S. Constitution the document, written and ratified in 1787, that established the framework of the national system of government that has continued to the present day.

ward someone, such as an orphan, who is under another person's protection or guardianship, often as a result of a legal action.

FURTHER INFORMATION

BOOKS

Drevitch, Gary. *Presidents FYI*. New York: HarperCollins Children's Books, 2008.

Gunderson, Megan M. *Andrew Jackson*. Edina, MN: ABDO, 2009.

Poulakidas, Georgene. *The War of 1812*. New York: PowerKids Press/ Primary Source, 2006.

DVD

Andrew Jackson: Good, Evil, and the Presidency. Dirs. Carl Byker, Mitchell Wilson. 2007. DVD. PBS Home Video, 2008.

WEBSITES

About the White House—Presidents: Andrew Jackson—1829–1837

www.whitehouse.gov/about/presidents/andrewjackson/

The official White House website detailing the life and accomplishments of the seventh president of the United States

The Hermitage—Home of President Andrew Jackson

www.thehermitage.com/

A site with a detailed overview of Jackson's famous Tennessee home, as well as a profile of his career and achievements

Tennessee History for Kids—Andrew Jackson

www.tnhistoryforkids.org/people/andrew_jackson

A website with a brief biography of Jackson and a link to a virtual tour of the Hermitage

BIBLIOGRAPHY

BOOKS

Anthony, Sferrazza Carl. *First Ladies: The Saga of the Presidents' Wives and Their Power, 1789–1961.* New York, HarperCollins, 1990.

Brady, Cyrus Townsend. *The True Andrew Jackson.* Philadelphia: Lippincott, 1906.

Brands, H. W. *Andrew Jackson, His Life and Times.* New York: Doubleday, 2005.

Buell, Augustus C. *History of Andrew Jackson—Pioneer, Patriot, Soldier, Politician, President.* New York: Scribner, 1904.

Meacham, Jon. *American Lion: Andrew Jackson in the White House.* New York: Random House, 2008.

Parton, James. *The Life of Andrew Jackson.* Boston: Houghton, Osgood, 1879.

Patterson, Benton Rain. *The Generals—Andrew Jackson, Sir Edward Pakenham, and the Road to the Battle of New Orleans.* New York: New York University Press, 2005.

Randall, Henry S. *The Life of Thomas Jefferson.* New York: Derby and Jackson, 1858.

Reid, John, and John Henry Eaton. *The Life of Andrew Jackson.* Edited by Frank L. Owsley Jr. Tuscaloosa: University of Alabama Press, 2007. First published 1817.

Remini, Robert V. *Andrew Jackson the Course of American Freedom, 1822–1832.* New York: Harper and Row, 1981.

———. *The Battle of New Orleans*. New York: Penguin, 2001. First published 1999 by Viking Penguin.

———. *The Life of Andrew Jackson*. New York: HarperCollins, 2001. First published 1988 by Harper and Row.

Wilentz, Sean. *Andrew Jackson*. New York: Times Books, 2005.

DVD

Andrew Jackson: Good, Evil, and the Presidency. Dirs. Carl Byker, Mitchell Wilson. 2007. DVD. PBS Home Video, 2008.

WEBSITES

About the White House—Presidents: Andrew Jackson—1829–1837
www.whitehouse.gov/about/presidents/andrewjackson/

American Heritage Magazine—Faces from the Past—V
www.americanheritage.com/articles/magazine/ah/1961/1/1961_1_16
.shtml

Biographical Directory of the United States Congress—
Jackson, Andrew
http://bioguide.congress.gov/scripts/biodisplay.pl?index=j000005

Bookmarks Magazine—American Lion: Andrew Jackson in the
White House
www.bookmarksmagazine.com/book-review/american-lion-andrew-
jackson-white-house/jon-meacham/

★ ★ ★ ★ ★ ★ ★ ★ ★ ★ ★ ★ ★ ★ ★ ★ ★ ★ ★

Columbia University—Speeches on the Passage of the Bill for the Removal of the Indians Delivered in the Congress of the United States
www.columbia.edu/~lmg21/BC3180/removal.html

C-SPAN—American Presidents: Life Portraits—Andrew Jackson
www.americanpresidents.org/presidents/president
   asp?PresidentNumber=7

Dave Leip's Atlas of U.S. Presidential Elections
www.uselectionatlas.org/

The Hermitage—Home of President Andrew Jackson
www.thehermitage.com/

Library of Congress—America's Story from America's Library—
Winning the Battle of New Orleans—January 8, 1815
www.americaslibrary.gov/cgi-bin/page.cgi/jb/nation/jackson_3

Miller Center of Public Affairs at the University of Virginia—
American President: Andrew Jackson
http://millercenter.org/academic/americanpresident/Jackson

Mount Holyoke College—International Relations Program:
"President Andrew Jackson's Case for the Removal Act,"
First Annual Message to Congress, 8 December 1830
www.mtholyoke.edu/acad/intrel/andrew.htm

MSN Encarta—Andrew Jackson
http://encarta.msn.com/encyclopedia_761569591/andrew_jackson.html

Northern Illinois University Libraries Digitalization Projects—Life on the
   Circuit with Lincoln, p. 526

http://lincoln.lib.niu.edu/cgi-bin/philologic/getobject.pl?p.3612:526.lincoln

State Library of North Carolina—Andrew Jackson

http://statelibrary.dcr.state.nc.us/nc/bio/public/Jackson.htm

University of Houston—Digital History: Jacksonian Democracy

www.digitalhistory.uh.edu/database/article_display.cfm?HHID=639

University of Pennsylvania—A Celebration of Women Writers:
Chapter 73, Jackson—"Liberty and Union, Now and Forever"—
Van Buren—Hard Times

http://digital.library.upenn.edu/women/marshall/country/
country-VII-73.html

Yale Law School—The Avalon Project: Andrew Jackson, First Inaugural
Address of Andrew Jackson

http://avalon.law.yale.edu/19th_century/jackson1.asp

★ ★ ★ ★ ★ ★ ★ ★ ★ ★ ★ ★ ★ ★ ★ ★ ★ ★ ★ ★

INDEX

Pages in **boldface** are illustrations.

ABOUT THE AUTHOR

Katie Marsico is the author of more than fifty reference books for children and young adults. Prior to becoming a full-time writer, Marsico worked as a managing editor in publishing. She resides near Chicago, Illinois, with her husband and three children.

★ ★ ★ ★ ★ ★ ★ ★ ★ ★ ★ ★ ★ ★ ★ ★ ★